Beattie

by Iain Gray

WRITING *to* REMEMBER

79 Main Street, Newtongrange,
Midlothian EH22 4NA
Tel: 0131 344 0414
E-mail: info@lang-syne.co.uk
www.langsyneshop.co.uk

Design by Dorothy Meikle
Printed by Printwell Ltd
© Lang Syne Publishers Ltd 2023

All rights reserved. No part of this publication may be reproduced, stored or introduced into a retrieval system, or transmitted in any form or by any means (electronic, mechanical, photocopying, recording or otherwise) without the prior written permission of Lang Syne Publishers Ltd.

ISBN 978-1-85217-779-9

Beattie

MOTTO:
May we follow heavenly inspiration

CREST:
A star issuing from a gold crescent

TERRITORY:
Dumfriesshire and the Borders

NAME variations include:
Batisoun
Baty
Betay
Beaty
Beattey
Beatie
Beatty
Betay
Bety

Chapter one:

The origins of the clan system

by Rennie McOwan

The original Scottish clans of the Highlands and the great families of the Lowlands and Borders were gatherings of families, relatives, allies and neighbours for mutual protection against rivals or invaders.

Scotland experienced invasion from the Vikings, the Romans and English armies from the south. The Norman invasion of what is now England also had an influence on land-holding in Scotland. Some of these invaders stayed on and in time became 'Scottish'.

The word clan derives from the Gaelic language term 'clann', meaning children, and it was first used many centuries ago as communities were formed around tribal lands in glens and mountain fastnesses.

The format of clans changed over the centuries, but at its best the chief and his family held the land on behalf of all, like trustees, and the ordinary clansmen and women believed they had a blood relationship with the founder of their clan.

There were two way duties and obligations. An inadequate chief could be deposed and replaced by someone of greater ability.

Clan people had an immense pride in race. Their relationship with the chief was like adult children to a father and they had a real dignity.

The concept of clanship is very old and a more feudal notion of authority gradually crept in.

Pictland, for instance, was divided into seven principalities ruled by feudal leaders who were the strongest and most charismatic leaders of their particular groups.

By the sixth century the 'British' kingdoms of Strathclyde, Lothian and Celtic Dalriada (Argyll) had emerged and Scotland, as one nation, began to take shape in the time of King Kenneth MacAlpin.

Some chiefs claimed descent from ancient kings which may not have been accurate in every case.

By the twelfth and thirteenth centuries the clans and families were more strongly brought under the central control of Scottish monarchs.

Lands were awarded and administered more and more under royal favour, yet the power of the area clan chiefs was still very great.

The long wars to ensure Scotland's

independence against the expansionist ideas of English monarchs extended the influence of some clans and reduced the lands of others.

Those who supported Scotland's greatest king, Robert the Bruce, were awarded the territories of the families who had opposed his claim to the Scottish throne.

In the Scottish Borders country – the notorious Debatable Lands – the great families built up a ferocious reputation for providing warlike men accustomed to raiding into England and occasionally fighting one another.

Chiefs had the power to dispense justice and to confiscate lands and clan warfare produced a society where martial virtues – courage, hardiness, tenacity – were greatly admired.

Gradually the relationship between the clans and the Crown became strained as Scottish monarchs became more orientated to life in the Lowlands and, on occasion, towards England.

The Highland clans spoke a different language, Gaelic, whereas the language of Lowland Scotland and the court was Scots and in more modern times, English.

Highlanders dressed differently, had different

customs, and their wild mountain land sometimes seemed almost foreign to people living in the Lowlands.

It must be emphasised that Gaelic culture was very rich and story-telling, poetry, piping, the clarsach (harp) and other music all flourished and were greatly respected.

Highland culture was different from other parts of Scotland but it was not inferior or less sophisticated.

Central Government, whether in London or Edinburgh, sometimes saw the Gaelic clans as a challenge to their authority and some sent expeditions into the Highlands and west to crush the power of the Lords of the Isles.

Nevertheless, when the eighteenth century Jacobite Risings came along the cause of the Stuarts was mainly supported by Highland clans.

The word Jacobite comes from the Latin for James – Jacobus. The Jacobites wanted to restore the exiled Stuarts to the throne of Britain.

The monarchies of Scotland and England became one in 1603 when King James VI of Scotland (1st of England) gained the English throne after Queen Elizabeth died.

The Union of Parliaments of Scotland and England, the Treaty of Union, took place in 1707.

Some Highland clans, of course, and Lowland families opposed the Jacobites and supported the incoming Hanoverians.

After the Jacobite cause finally went down at Culloden in 1746 a kind of ethnic cleansing took place. The power of the chiefs was curtailed. Tartan and the pipes were banned in law.

Many emigrated, some because they wanted to, some because they were evicted by force. In addition, many Highlanders left for the cities of the south to seek work.

Many of the clan lands became home to sheep and deer shooting estates.

But the warlike traditions of the clans and the great Lowland and Border families lived on, with their descendants fighting bravely for freedom in two world wars.

Remember the men from whence you came, says the Gaelic proverb, and to that could be added the role of many heroic women.

The spirit of the clan, of having roots, whether Highland or Lowland, means much to thousands of people.

Meanwhile, many families proudly boast the heraldic device known as a Coat of Arms, as featured on our front cover.

The central motif of the Coat of Arms would originally have been what was sometimes borne on the shield of a warrior to distinguish himself from others on the battlefield.

Not featured on the Coat of Arms, but highlighted on page three, is the family motto and related crest – with the latter frequently different from the central motif.

Clan warfare produced a society where courage and tenacity were greatly admired

Chapter two:

Moss troopers

A name long associated with the borderlands of Scotland and England, 'Beattie' and its numerous spelling variants derives from 'Bate' or 'Baty' – diminutives of what was the popular forename 'Bartholomew'.

This, in turn, denoted a 'public victualler' or someone who held land on condition they supplied food to those billeted on them from time to time by a clan chief or other tribal leader.

Dumfriesshire and the adjoining Borders are where the name is first recorded in Scotland, and Beattie tradition holds that their forefathers who first settled there were Anglo-Saxons from across the border in what was then the vast territory of Northumbria.

This means that flowing through the veins of many bearers of the Beattie name today may well be the blood of those Germanic tribes who invaded and settled in Britain from about the early fifth century.

Known as the Anglo-Saxons, they were composed of the Jutes, from the area of the Jutland

Peninsula in modern Denmark, the Saxons from Lower Saxony, in modern Germany and the Angles from the Angeln area.

It was the Angles who gave the name 'Engla land', or 'Aengla land' – better known as 'England.'

They held sway from approximately 550 to 1066, with the main kingdoms those of Sussex, Wessex, Northumbria, Mercia, Kent, East Anglia and Essex.

The influx of Anglo-Saxons such as the Beatties into Scotland came in the aftermath of a vicious purge launched against them and Danish settlers and their followers by William the Conqueror, victor of the battle of Hastings in 1066.

Following his defeat of King Harold II, William was declared monarch and the complete subjugation of his subjects followed, with those Normans who had fought on his behalf rewarded with lands.

But trouble brewed for the conqueror in the north of his new realm, where rebellions had been stirred by Edgar Atheling, claimant to the former kingdom of Wessex.

In 'The Harrying of the North', William's response was brutal – laying waste from 1069 to 1070 to the northern shires, including the city of York and replacing native aristocracy and their followers – such as those who would come to bear the Beattie name in Scotland – with Normans deemed more loyal.

In 1071, King Malcolm III of Scotland married Margaret, a sister of the Saxon Edgar Atheling and therefore had an affinity with the dispossessed northerners – welcoming them to settle in his realm.

Future monarchs may well have had cause to regret this, however, because the Beatties were among the feared body of families known as riding clans, or reivers.

They took this name from their time-honoured custom of reiving, or raiding, not only their neighbours' livestock but also that of their counterparts across the border – while the word 'bereaved', for example, indicating to have suffered loss, derives from the original 'reived', meaning loss of property.

A constant thorn in the flesh of both the English and Scottish authorities was the cross-border raiding and pillaging carried out by well-mounted and heavily armed men, the contingent from the Scottish side known and feared as 'moss troopers' or 'freebooters'.

In an attempt to bring order to what was known as the wild 'debateable land' on both sides of the border, King Alexander II of Scotland had in 1237 signed the Treaty of York, which for the first time established the Scottish border with England as a line running from the Solway to the Tweed.

On either side of the border there were three 'marches' or areas of administration, the West, East, and Middle Marches, and a warden governed these.

Complaints from either side of the border were dealt with on Truce Days, when the wardens of the different marches would act as arbitrators.

There was also a law known as the Hot Trod, that granted anyone who had their livestock stolen the right to pursue the thieves and recover their property.

The post of March Warden was a powerful and lucrative one, with rival families vying for the position, and the marches became virtually a law unto themselves.

In the Scottish borderlands, the Homes and Swintons dominated the East March, while the Armstrongs, Maxwells, Johnstones and Grahams were the rulers of the West March – also the domain of the Beatties – while the Kerrs, along with the Douglases and Elliots, held sway in the Middle March.

Wardens from the East Marches met at Redden Burn, on the Tweed, just west of Wark, while wardens for the Middle Marches met at Deadwater, on the North Tyne.

A record exists from 1398 of an agreement between commissioners for Scotland and England that the men of Nithsdale, Galloway, Crawfordmuir and Annandale should meet the wardens of the West March at the 'Clochmabanstane' for redress.

Also known as the Lochmaben Stone, or the Clochmaben Stone, this granite bulk was situated about a mile southwest of Gretna, on a small rise of ground at the head of the Solway Firth, at Sulwath.

For the reivers such as the Beatties, however, their freebooting lifestyle was simply a means of survival, summed up by the philosophy:

The freebooter ventures both life and limb
Good wife, and bairn, and every other thing;
He must do so, or else must starve and die,
For all his livelihood comes of the enemy.

In an act that proved mutually beneficial to some reiving families and the Crown, in 1455 the Beatties – along with others including the Scotts, Maxwells and Johnstones – helped King James II crush the power of his powerful rivals the Black Douglases.

This was at the battle of Arkinholm, near Langholm, where Archibald Douglas was slain and his head proudly presented to the triumphant king.

For their service to the Crown, the Beatties were rewarded with lands that saw them gain a secure foothold in the Langholm and Eskdale areas.

But they appear to have fallen from grace just under 50 years later when, in 1504, Adam Batie was hanged for being part of "the king's rebels at Eskdale", while in 1537 they were deprived by King James V of their Eskdale lands in favour of Lord Robert Maxwell.

Refusing to acknowledge Maxwell as their feudal superior, the Beatties prepared to launch an attack against him.

Nevertheless, and perhaps through some code of honour peculiar to the Borderers, Ronald Beattie, chief of the clan, provided him with a fast horse to escape slaughter.

Lord Maxwell subsequently sold the former Beattie lands to the warden of the Middle March, who was of the Scott clan – but Maxwell successfully appealed to him to reward Ronald Beattie for having saved his life.

Again, honour appears to have prevailed, as

or leader, Muhammad Ahmad bin Abd Allah, he was commended for his actions with the award of the Distinguished Service Order (DSO).

Promoted to captain in recognition of his actions in China during the Boxer Rebellion between 1889 and 1901, he returned to Britain for treatment to an arm injury received in combat.

It was while recuperating and out hunting that, by chance, he met and fell in love with Ethel Tree, daughter and heiress of the wealthy Chicago department store founder Marshall Field.

For Beatty, one of Ethel's attractions as a wife – in addition to her attractive looks and as an heiress – was also her ability as a huntress, but there was a problem.

Ethel was already married – but Beatty, used to overcoming obstacles, somehow managed to charm her hapless husband, Ronald Tree, into agreeing to co-operate.

Accordingly, he filed for divorce on the grounds of desertion and, this granted, the seafarer and the heiress married in May of 1901.

The significant financial independence this brought him allowed him to act as a law unto himself and, on one occasion when threatened with serious disciplinary action for putting undue strain on his ship's engines, his doting wife commented:

"What? Court-martial my David? I'll buy them a new ship."

Promoted to Rear-Admiral Commanding the 1st Battlecruiser Squadron in March of 1913 and later to Vice-Admiral, he led them in three famous First World War naval actions.

At the battle of Heligoland Bight, more properly the First Battle of Heligoland Bight and the

David Richard Beatty, 1st Earl Beatty.

first naval action of the war, on August 28, 1914, the British Grand Fleet attacked patrols of the German High Seas Fleet in the south-eastern North Sea.

A flotilla of five battlecruisers commanded by Beatty, 31 destroyers, six cruisers and six light cruisers, sank three German light cruisers and one destroyer, with three British destroyers and one light cruiser destroyed.

Beatty was hailed a hero for his role in the battle – although some of his detractors later pointed out he had taken no part in the planning of the action.

At the battle of Dogger Bank in the North Sea on January 25, 1915, Beattie's battlecruisers were again in action when the German heavy cruiser *Blücher* was sunk.

But the engagement for which he gained particular fame was the battle of Jutland, fought off the North Sea coast of Denmark's Jutland Peninsula from May 31 to June 1, 1916.

With the British fleet under the overall command of Admiral Sir John Jellicoe and in what is recognised as the last major naval battle in history fought primarily by battleships, the Germans had attempted to lure out, trap and destroy the fleet.

Involving a number of separate engagements,

with vessels zig-zagging across the sea, guns blazing, Beatty's battlecruiser force engaged with one commanded by Vice-Admiral Franz Hipper, both suffering casualties.

As the dense smoke and cordite fumes from hundreds of high velocity shells eventually dissipated, fourteen British and eleven German vessels had sank beneath the oil-slicked waves, with a combined loss of 9,823 lives.

Debate continues to this day over which side, if any, was actually 'victorious', but the British had succeeded in containing the German fleet and it would never again be a serious force to be reckoned with.

The battle also sealed Beatty's reputation and, in December of 1916, he was promoted to Admiral and, at the end of the war, to Admiral of the Fleet.

Created 1st Earl Beatty in 1919 and also First Sea Lord, he retired from naval service in 1927, nine years before his death in 1936, his wife having predeceased him in 1932.

The father of two sons, the eldest, David Beatty, 2nd Earl Beatty, was the Royal Navy officer and Conservative Party politician born in 1905 and who died in 1972 having served for a time at the end of the Second World War as Under-Secretary of State for Air.

His younger brother, born in 1910, was the flamboyant English racehorse owner and breeder, businessman and socialite Peter Beatty.

With his main residence the magnificent Mereworth Castle, Kent, where he frequently played host to international celebrities including Prince Aly Khan and his first wife the American actress Rita Hayworth, he was nicknamed 'Lucky' because of his success in breeding winning racehorses.

One tale he was fond of relating to friends was that he had once consulted a fortune teller who told him he would win the Epsom Derby with a horse with the letter 's' recurring thrice in its name.

Four years later, in 1938, he won the Derby with his horse Bois Roussel.

Although described by contemporaries as classically 'tall, dark and handsome' and considered at one point Britain's most eligible bachelor, he had suffered from an early age from the debilitating eye disease *ophthalmia neonatorum*.

His sight steadily deteriorated until, in 1949, he was told he would soon go totally blind.

Shortly afterwards, in October of that year,

he fell to his death from the sixth storey of the Ritz Hotel in London, where he had been staying.

The coroner's verdict was that he had committed suicide – one theory being that he could not bear the thought of no longer being able to see his beloved racehorses.

Returning to the high seas, and during the Second World War, Captain Stephen Beattie, born in 1908 at Leighton, Montgomeryshire, was the Welsh recipient of the Victoria Cross (VC) – the highest reward for valour in the face of enemy action for British and Commonwealth forces.

He had been a lieutenant-commander in the Royal Navy when, during the successful raid to destroy the dry dock at St Nazaire, Normandy, on March 8, 1942, and in command of HMS *Campbeltown*, he deliberately rammed the vessel under extreme German fire into the dock's lock-gates.

Taken prisoner after grounding the ship and spending the remainder of the conflict in a prisoner-of-war camp, he was later awarded the VC in recognition of not only his own valour but also that of his crew.

He died in 1975, while his medal is now on display at the Imperial War Museum, London.

Chapter four:

On the world stage

Bearers of the Beattie name and its popular spelling variants have gained recognition through a diverse range of endeavours and pursuits.

A veteran of the Scottish entertainment scene, **Johnny Beattie** was the stand-up comedian and actor born into a working class family in the Govan area of Glasgow in 1926.

Leaving school when aged sixteen intending to take up a trade apprenticeship, he became diverted by amateur dramatics and discovered a talent for the stage as a comedian.

By the mid-1950s he had established a career as a comic stand-up, and this transferred to the television screen in 1964 through the BBC Scotland series *Johnny Beattie's Saturday Night Show*.

This ran until 1970 and in 1974 he starred beside Stanley Baxter, Mark McManus, Rikki Fulton, Jack Milroy and Billy Connolly in the STV series *A Grand Tour*.

Famous for his character 'Glaikit O'Toole', other comedy series he appeared in include *Scotch and Wry* and *Rab C. Nesbitt*, while also hosting for a time the game show *Now You See It*.

Big screen credits include the 1990 *The Big Man*, starring beside Liam Neeson and Billy Connolly while, from 2002 until his retirement from show business in 2015, he played the role of the pensioner Malcolm Hamilton in the popular BBC Scotland soap *River City*.

The recipient of awards and honours including an OBE, he died in 2020.

Through his marriage to the late Kitty Lamont he was the father of two sons and two daughters.

His eldest daughter, Maureen Beattie, is the actress who was born in 1953 in Bundoran, Co. Donegal while her father was performing on stage in Ireland.

After studying at the Royal Scottish Academy of Music and Drama (RSAMD), Glasgow, she quickly established a reputation as an accomplished stage actress.

Having played with theatre companies including National Theatre of Scotland, the National Theatre of Great Britain and the Royal Shakespeare Company – including in the role of the Duchess of

York in a production of *Richard II* – she has also starred on the small screen in a number of series.

These include the medical drama *Casualty*, police drama *The Bill*, *Bramwell* and *A Wing and a Prayer*, while big screen credits include the 2007 *Finding Bob McArthur*.

The recipient of an OBE for services to the entertainment industry and elected president of the actors' trade union Equity in 2018, her younger sister is the actress and writer **Louise Beattie**.

Born in Glasgow in 1964, her television credits include *Emmerdale*, *Naked Video*, *Taggart* and *Blood Red Roses*.

Across the Atlantic, Henry Warren Beaty is the award-winning American actor and filmmaker better known by his stage name **Warren Beatty**.

Born in 1937 in Richmond, Virginia, his film credits include the 1961 *Splendor in the Grass*, the 1967 *Bonnie and Clyde*, the 1975 *Shampoo* and the 1981 *Reds* – which he also produced and which won him the Academy Award for Best Director, Adapted Screenplay.

With a number of other awards including six Golden Globes and the Irving G. Thalberg Award, the highest honour bestowed by the Academy of

Motion Picture Arts and Sciences, he is a younger brother of Shirley MacLean Beaty, better known as the actress and singer **Shirley MacLaine**.

Born in 1934 and the recipient in 2012 of the American Film Institute's Life Achievement Award and the 1998 Golden Globe Cecil B. DeMille Award, her screen credits include the 1958 *Some Came Running*, the 1983 *Terms of Endearment*, for which she won the Academy Award for Best Actress, the 1989 *Steel Magnolias* and, from 2011, *Bernie*.

Still on American shores, **Ned Beatty** is the retired actor and singer whose career spanned more than 160 films and who is the recipient of numerous awards and Academy Award nominations.

These are for memorable roles in films including the 1972 *Deliverance*, the 1976 *All the President's Men*, the 1978 *Superman*, the 1987 *The Fourth Protocol* and, from 2007, *Charlie Wilson's War*.

Lending his voice to animated films, his credits include 'Lots-O'-Huggin'-Bear' in the 2010 *Toy Story 3* and 'Tortoise John' in the 2011 *Rango*.

Back on British shores, **Joseph Beattie** is the television and film actor born in 1978.

With big screen credits including the 1994

The Browning Version, the 1998 *Velvet Goldmine* and the 2008 *Brideshead Revisited*, his television portfolio includes *Tom Brown's Schooldays*, *Hex* and *Mansfield Park*.

Behind the camera lens, **John Watt Beattie** was the Scots-born photographer who captured enduring images for posterity of Tasmania.

Born in 1859 in Aberdeen and later immigrating to Australia, he was appointed Photographer to the Government of Tasmania in 1896 and, in addition to taking images for its archives, toured with popular lantern-slide shows with subjects including *A trip through Tasmania*.

Some of his photographs, such as *Port Arthur* and *Isle of the Dead*, were used on postcards well into the twentieth century, while also serving as aids in campaigns for the protection of nature.

A Fellow of the Royal Society of Tasmania, he died in 1930.

Bearers of the Beattie name have also excelled in the highly competitive world of sport.

Born in 1957 in North Borneo, where his father managed a rubber estate, but returning to Scotland with his family when aged eleven, **John Beattie** is the former rugby union player who now enjoys a career as a pundit for the game and broadcaster in general.

Showing an early aptitude for rugby with teams including Glasgow Schoolboys and Glasgow Academicals, he progressed as a No. 8 to win a total of 25 caps for Scotland, with his first try for his nation in 1987 against France.

Also having toured twice with the British Lions and coached teams including Glasgow Academicals and West of Scotland, his playing career ended because of a knee injury.

A qualified civil engineer and chartered accountant, his career followed a much different path in 1995 by moving to broadcasting.

A rugby presenter and commentator on both radio and television, he also hosts a BBC Radio Scotland news, comment and discussion programme and, from 2019, has co-presented the television news programme *The Nine*.

A former chairman of a Scottish government taskforce to improve the health of the nation, he is the father of the former rugby union international John Beattie, better known as **Johnnie Beattie**, born in Glasgow in 1985.

A No. 8, in common with his father, and the

recipient of 38 caps with his nation, teams he has played for include Glasgow Warriors and French teams Montpellier, Castres and Bayonne.

He retired from the game in 2020, while he is the older brother of the Scottish football international **Jennifer Beattie**, born in 1991.

First kicking a ball with her brother and his friends while still at primary school, she started her professional career in the Scottish Women's Premier League with Glasgow team Queen's Park.

In addition to playing for her country, other teams she has played for include Celtic Ladies, Arsenal Ladies and Manchester City Women.

Still on the football pitch, **Frank Beattie**, born in 1933 in St Ninian's, Stirling, was the player and manager who spent his senior career between 1954 and 1972 playing for Kilmarnock.

Captain of the team when it won the 1964-65 Scottish league championship and having managed Albion Rovers and Stirling Albion, he died in 2009.

The Frank Beattie Stand at Kilmarnock's Rugby Park stadium is named in his honour.

In contemporary Scottish football, **Craig Beattie**, born in Glasgow in 1984, is the striker who has played at international level and for clubs including Elgin City, Hearts, Swansea City, St Johnstone and Stirling Albion.

Across the border, **James Beattie**, born in Lancaster in 1978, is the English former footballer who played for teams including Blackburn Rovers, Everton, Sheffield United and Rangers, in addition to his national team.

As a coach, he has worked with teams including Leeds United and Birmingham City, while **Kevin Beattie**, born in Carlisle in 1953 and who died in 2018, was one of the Ipswich Town players cast in the 1981 film *Escape to Victory*.

In the much different sport of skiing, **Bob Beattie** was the American promoter and commentator born in 1933 in Manchester, New Hampshire.

Co-founder of the Alpine Skiing World Cup in 1966 and head coach of the U.S. Ski Team from 1961 to 1969 and the recipient in 1997 of the International Ski Federation's Journalist Award, he died in 2018.

From sport to the world of the written word, **Ann Beattie**, born in 1947 in Washington, D.C., is the American novelist and short story writer whose novels include the 1976 *Chilly Scenes of Winter*, adapted for film, and the 2019 *A Wonderful Stroke of Luck*.

Writing when the world was on the cusp of the Space Age, **Jerome M. Beatty, Jr.**, born in 1916 and who died in 2002, was the American author best known for his *Matthew and Maria Looney* series of science fiction books for children.

Also a noted feature writer for magazines, his popular science fiction series – first published in the early 1960s and before the famous Moon landing in 1969 – depict a brother and sister who, despite being born there, are uncannily similar in behaviour to children on Earth.